T0072056

Gluten-Free

MINIATURE DESSERTS

TARTLETS, MINI PIES, CAKE POPS, AND MORE

ABIGAIL R. GEHRING

Skyhorse Publishing

With gratitude to my husband, Tim Lawrence, whose culinary creations nourish and inspire me and who contributed several recipes for this book.

Copyright © 2013 by Abigail R. Gehring

All Rights Reserved. No part of this book may be reproduced in any manner without the express written consent of the publisher, except in the case of brief excerpts in critical reviews or articles. All inquiries should be addressed to Skyhorse Publishing, 307 West 36th Street, 11th Floor, New York, NY 10018.

Skyhorse Publishing books may be purchased in bulk at special discounts for sales promotion, corporate gifts, fund-raising, or educational purposes. Special editions can also be created to specifications. For details, contact the Special Sales Department, Skyhorse Publishing, 307 West 36th Street, 11th Floor, New York, NY 10018 or info@skyhorsepublishing.com.

Skyhorse® and Skyhorse Publishing® are registered trademarks of Skyhorse Publishing, Inc.®, a Delaware corporation.

Visit our website at www.skyhorsepublishing.com.

10 9 8 7 6 5 4 3 2 1

Library of Congress Cataloging-in-Publication Data is available on file.
ISBN: 978-1-62636-024-2

Printed in China

{ Contents }

The Gluten-Free Kitchen   vii

Cakes, Cupcakes, and Cake Pops   1

Pies, Crisps, and Tartlets   29

Mousses, Puddings, and Parfaits   67

Sorbets, Popsicles, and Frozen Treats   87

Cookies and Candies   99

Fruits, Nuts, Meringues, and Other Light Treats   111

Index   125

Conversion Charts   128

{ The Gluten-Free Kitchen }

If there's anything lucky about having celiac disease or gluten-sensitivity, it's that we have it now, when the availability of gluten-free products is expanding at lightning speed. As few as five years ago, many folks didn't even know what gluten was, and unless you were in a natural foods store or specialty grocery store, you wouldn't be likely to see a single item labeled "gluten-free." Now, many mainstream supermarkets have whole gluten-free sections, and many restaurants provide gluten-free menus! (Though, a word of warning: gluten-free menus are not always as exciting as they seem. I once ordered eggs benedict from a gluten-free menu, eagerly awaiting the first English muffin I'd had since discovering gluten made me feel lousy. When the plate arrived with just a lonely poached egg and a bit of hollandaise sauce—*sans* English muffin—I was sorely disappointed.) Going gluten-free is a whole lot easier now than it ever has been before. Still, it takes some time to recognize which ingredients are safe and which are not, and there is the unavoidable fact that gluten holds baked goods together and helps them rise and without it, your cookies, cakes, and piecrusts are at a high risk of being flat and crumbling to bits. Those are really two separate issues, so let's start with the first one: ingredients.

Ingredients to Avoid

Wheat, rye, and barley are the gluten-laden culprits you must avoid. Unfortunately, that's not as simple as it sounds, since those three grains show up in a myriad of forms. Here's a list of common dessert ingredients to watch out for:

DANGER LIST
Barley, barley malt, barley extract
Bran
Bread flour
Bulgur wheat
Cereal
Durum
Einkorn
Farina
Farro
Gluten
Graham flour
Kamut
Malt extract, malt flavoring, malt syrup
Matzo
Oats, oat bran, oat fiber, oat syrup*
Rice Syrup, brown rice syrup **
Rye
Semolina
Spelt***
Sprouted wheat
Wheat, wheat berry, wheat bran, wheat germ, wheat grass, wheat starch, wheat berries

* Oats are often processed in facilities that also process wheat. Look for certified gluten-free oats to ensure they're safe.

** Rice syrup is often processed using barley enzymes. Check with the manufacturer to ensure the brand you use is safe.

*** Spelt is an ancient variety of wheat, so it is not safe for individuals with celiac disease. However, some people with gluten-sensitivity or intolerance find that they can tolerate spelt just fine.

To further complicate things, these ingredients can show up in some unexpected places. The below ingredients do not always contain gluten and when they do it's trace amounts, but especially if you have celiac disease, you should be careful about what brand of the following items you are buying. Look for ones that are specifically labeled "gluten-free."

MAYBE LIST
Alcohol
Artificial color
Baking powder
Brewer's yeast
Chocolate
Dextrin
Dextrimaltose
Dry roasted nuts
Flavoring and flavor extracts
Glucose syrup
Ground spices
Instant coffee
Maltose
Modfied food starch
Non-dairy creamer

Now for the good news. There are lots of flours, starches, and other essential dessert ingredients that you *can* eat. Here I'll focus on the flours and starches, since those are the trickiest areas. The following are safe to eat on a gluten-free diet:

SAFE LIST
Agar-agar
Almond flour
Amaranth
Arrowroot flour or starch
Buckwheat flour
Cashew flour
Chestnut flour
Chickpea/garbanzo flour
Coconut flour
Cornmeal and cornstarch
Flaxseeds
Gelatin
Millet flour
Oats (if they're certified gluten-free)
Pecan flour
Potato flour
Potato starch
Quinoa
Rice flour, brown rice flour, sweet rice flour
Sorghum
Soy flour
Sweet potato/yam flour
Tapioca flour and tapioca starch
Teff flour
Xanthan gum

Tips for Successful Gluten-Free Baking

- Use a mix of flours and starches. On page xii you'll find a basic recipe for gluten-free all-purpose flour. It includes a variety of flours and starches, which helps to ensure a nice texture in your finished dessert. Using sweet rice flour adds some "stickiness" to your batter or dough that is sometimes lacking in gluten-free flours. I recommend brown sweet rice flour (rather than white), since it's a bit more nutritious. (Note: sweet rice flour is sometimes called "sweet rice glutinous flour," but it doesn't contain any gluten.)

- Go small (obviously a big theme in this book). Smaller cakes, muffins, and cookies hang together more easily than really big ones.

- Add moisture. Applesauce, pumpkin puree, and yogurt add moisture and nutrition to gluten-free baked goods. Using brown sugar instead of white also helps, as does using a little honey or gluten-free brown rice syrup.

- Chill your cookie dough. Gluten-free cookie dough tends to spread out a lot. This will happen less if you drop your cookie dough onto the pan and then stick the whole pan in the refrigerator for half an hour or so before baking.

- Darker baking pans will lead to better browning.

- Store your baked goods in the refrigerator or freezer to keep them from getting stale.

- One man's baking disaster is another man's gorgeous trifle. There are plenty of good uses for baked goods that fall apart, including trifles (page 82) and cake pops (page 2).

XANTHAN GUM

When I first discovered xanthan gum, I thought it was brilliant. A dash of the powdery white stuff and suddenly my cookies became moist and held their shape almost perfectly. But that was before I realized that combining various flours can lend similar results and more nutrition. Do I think xanthan gum is bad? No, it's actually pretty handy stuff, and a little bit goes a long way in cakes and cookies. But it's expensive and not entirely necessary for most baked goods, so if you decide to skip it when it appears in the recipes in this book, don't fret—you should still end up with a perfectly good finished product.

All-Purpose Gluten-Free Flour Mix

- 2 cups brown rice flour or brown sweet rice flour
- 2 cups sorghum flour
- 2 cups potato starch, tapioca flour, or arrowroot powder (choose two types of starch to combine for best results)

Sorghum flour is high in protein and fiber and has a lovely slight sweetness to it. I love it in baked goods, but for a slightly grainier texture you can also experiment with replacing the sorghum in this all-purpose mix with buckwheat, almond flour, coconut flour, or a mix of these.

{ Cakes, Cupcakes, and Cake Pops }

Cake Pops   2

Peanut Butter Cheesecake Pops   5

Lemon Cheesecake Bites with Blueberry-Lemon Sauce   6

Mini Pumpkin Cheesecakes with Gingersnap Crust   8

Chocolate-Orange Cheesecake Bites   10

Chocolate Volcano Cakes   12

Lemon Coconut Petit Fours   13

Mini Carrot Cakes   15

Mini Gingerbread Pumpkin Cupcakes with Spiced Cream   17

Mini Chocolate Bundt Cakes with Sour Cream Glaze   19

Cranberry Pound Cake with Lemon Glaze   21

Lemon Poundcake with
    Fruit and Cream   24

Almond Bundt Cake with Chocolate Glaze   26

Cake Pops

MAKES A DOZEN CAKE POPS

Ingredients

12 lollipip sticks

CAKE

1½ cups gluten-free all-purpose
   flour

¾ cup cocoa powder

½ cup granulated sugar

½ cup brown sugar

½ teaspoon salt

1 teaspoon baking soda

1 teaspoon baking powder

2 teaspoons xanthan gum

¾ cup butter, softened,
   or coconut oil

3 eggs

1 teaspoon vanilla

1½ cups buttermilk (or 1 cup milk
   mixed with 1 teaspoon vinegar
   and allowed to sit for a few minutes until curdled)

FILLING (choose one)

Coconut:

1 can full-fat coconut milk, chilled

Peanut butter:

½ cup peanut butter

½ cup cream cheese

3 tablespoons confectioners' sugar

Chocolate:

½ cup chocolate frosting

COATING

3 ounces chocolate chips

1 tablespoon butter

Directions

1. Preheat the oven to 350°F. Grease two 9-inch cake pans.

Continued on page 4

2. Combine all the dry ingredients and mix. Add the butter or oil, eggs, vanilla, and buttermilk and beat until smooth.

3. Divide batter between the two pans and bake for about 30 minutes or until a toothpick inserted into the cakes comes out clean. Remove from oven and allow cakes to cool.

4. Crumble both cakes into a large mixing bowl. Use your hands or a mixer to break the cakes apart until you have a pile of coarse cake crumbs. Add your filling of choice and continue to mix until the pieces start to cling together. Adjust the amount of filling if necessary, being careful not to make the mixture too goopy.

5. Roll mixture into balls, place on a cookie sheet, and freeze for about ten minutes. Remove from freezer and insert sticks.

6. Melt the chocolate in a double boiler and dip each cake pop into the melted chocolate. Stick them into a stiff piece of styrofoam to hold them upright while they dry. If desired, pipe with a contrasting color of frosting or roll in colored sugar.

> You can find lollipop sticks at craft or specialty cooking stores, or you can cut traditional wooden skewers into shorter lengths (trimming off the sharp points), or use wooden chopsticks instead.

Peanut Butter Cheesecake Pops

MAKES ABOUT 24

Ingredients

---

1 (8-ounce) package cream cheese

1 cup smooth peanut butter

2 teaspoons lemon juice

1 pint heavy whipping cream

⅓ cup white sugar

12 ounces chocolate chips

24 lollipop sticks

Sprinkles or small candies
  (optional)

Directions

1. In a medium bowl, beat together the cream cheese, peanut butter, and lemon juice. Add the heavy whipping cream and continue to beat until batter thickens. Add the sugar, and keep beating. When batter is stiff, cover and chill for 6 hours or overnight.

2. Line two baking sheets with parchment paper. Use a small cookie scoop or your hands to roll the cheesecake batter into balls, placing them on the cookie sheet. Place the tray in the freezer for about 2 hours.

3. Melt the chocolate in a double boiler. Dip each ball in the chocolate and then scoop it out with a spoon. Immediately roll in sprinkles or candies (if using), and then place them on the second lined cookie sheet. Work quickly, but make sure they're fully coated. Place a lollipop stick in each ball and refrigerate about 10 minutes to set the chocolate. Serve, or store in an airtight container in the refrigerator for up to a week.

Lemon Cheesecake Bites with Blueberry-Lemon Sauce

MAKES ABOUT 48 MINI CHEESECAKES

Ingredients

CRUST

1½ cups crushed gluten-free graham crackers (9–10 crackers)

4 tablespoons butter, melted

FILLING

2 (8-ounce) packages cream cheese, softened

⅔ cup granulated sugar

2 eggs

1 teaspoon lemon zest

1 tablespoon fresh squeezed lemon juice

¼ teaspoon vanilla extract

TOPPING

2 cups fresh blueberries, divided

¼ cup sugar

1 tablespoon cornstarch

3 tablespoons freshly squeezed lemon juice

2 teaspoons lemon zest

½ teaspoon vanilla extract

Directions

1. Preheat oven to 350°F. Line two mini muffin tins with paper liners.

2. In a medium mixing bowl, combine the graham cracker crumbs with the butter and mix until dough hangs together. Place about 1 teaspoon of crust batter into each paper liner and press down firmly. You can use your fingers or a pestle (from a mortar and pestle) to help. Bake for about 8 minutes. Remove from oven and allow to cool while you prepare the filling.

3. Cream together the cream cheese, sugar, eggs, lemon zest, lemon juice, and vanilla. Spoon the mixture into the crusts, filling the paper liners just about all the way. Bake for about 15 minutes or until the fillings are set. Transfer to a rack to cool. Refrigerate for about an hour.

4. To make the topping, in a medium saucepan whisk together the sugar and cornstarch. Add one cup of blueberries, the lemon juice, lemon zest, and vanilla, and turn the heat to low. Simmer until the berries soften and the sauce begins to thicken (about 8 minutes). Add the remaining cup of blueberries and cook another 5 minutes or so.

5. You can leave the cheesecakes in their paper liners, or remove the liners before garnishing with the berry sauce. Spoon the mixture over the cheesecakes and serve. Store leftovers in a sealed container in the refrigerator for 5–6 days.

Gluten-free graham crackers are available in many grocery stores (especially health food stores) or online. Or you can make your own (see page 103).

Mini Pumpkin Cheesecakes with Gingersnap Crust

MAKES ABOUT 48 MINI CHEESECAKES

Ingredients

CRUST

1 cup gluten-free gingersnap crumbs

½ cup almond flour

1 tablespoon molasses

1 tablespoon brown sugar

½ cup unsalted butter, melted

FILLING

2 (8-ounce) packages cream cheese

1 cup pumpkin puree

2 eggs

½ cup sugar

¼ cup heavy cream

1 teaspoon vanilla

½ teaspoon cinnamon

½ teaspoon pumpkin pie spice or allspice

MAPLE WHIPPED CREAM

2 cups heavy cream

2 tablespoons maple syrup

Directions

1. Preheat oven to 350°F. Line two mini muffin tins with paper liners.

2. In a medium mixing bowl or food processor, combine the gingersnap crumbs, almond flour, molasses, brown sugar, and butter and mix until dough hangs together. Place about 1 teaspoon of crust batter into each paper liner and press down firmly. You can use your fingers or a pestle (from a mortar and pestle) to help. Bake for about 8 minutes. Remove from oven and allow to cool while you prepare the filling.

3. Cream together the cream cheese, pumpkin puree, and eggs until smooth. Add the sugar, heavy cream, vanilla, and spices and mix just until combined. Spoon the mixture into the crusts, filling the

paper liners just about all the way. Bake for about 20 minutes or until the fillings are set. Transfer to a rack to cool. Refrigerate for about two hours.

4. To make the whipped cream, in a large bowl, beat the heavy cream until it forms peaks. Add maple syrup and continue beating until desired consistency is reached. If you want the whipped cream to hold its shape when squirted onto the cheesecakes, keep whipping until you're approaching whipped butter consistency.

5. You can leave the cheesecakes in their paper liners, or remove the liners before garnishing with the whipped cream. (Don't add the whipped cream until just before serving.) Use a spoon to dollop some on each cheesecake, or squirt from a pastry bag with a star-shaped top to create a pretty swirl. Store leftovers in a sealed container in the refrigerator for 5–6 days.

Gluten-free gingersnap cookies are widely available in grocery stores, health food stores, or online. To turn the cookies into crumbs, place them in a ziplock bag and using a rolling pin to crush them.

Chocolate-Orange Cheesecake Bites

MAKES ABOUT 48 MINI CHEESECAKES

Ingredients

CRUST

1½ cups crushed gluten-free graham crackers (9–10 crackers)

4 tablespoons butter, melted

2 tablespoons cocoa powder

8 ounces mini chocolate chips

FILLING

2 (8-ounce) packages cream cheese, softened

⅔ cup granulated sugar

2 eggs

2 teaspoons orange zest

1 tablespoon fresh squeezed orange juice

¼ teaspoon almond extract

TOPPING

2 tablespoons orange zest

2 tablespoons sugar

Directions

1. Preheat oven to 350°F. Line two mini muffin tins with paper liners.

2. In a medium mixing bowl, combine the graham cracker crumbs with the butter and cocoa powder and mix until dough hangs together. Place about 1 teaspoon of crust batter into each paper liner and press down firmly. You can use your fingers or a pestle (from a mortar and pestle) to help. Bake for about 8 minutes. Remove from oven and allow to cool while you prepare the filling.

3. Cream together the cream cheese, sugar, eggs, orange zest, orange juice, and almond extract.

4. Sprinkle the baked crusts with the mini chocolate chips. Then spoon the filling mixture on top, filling the paper liners just about

all the way. Bake for about 15 minutes or until the fillings are set. Transfer to a rack to cool. Refrigerate for about an hour.

5. You can leave the cheesecakes in their paper liners, or remove the liners before garnishing with the topping. To make the topping, combine the orange zest and sugar and sprinkle over the cheesecakes.

Gluten-free graham crackers are available in many grocery stores (especially health food stores) or online. Or you can make your own (see page 103).

Chocolate Volcano Cakes

MAKES 6 INDIVIDUAL CAKES

Ingredients

8 ounces bittersweet chocolate, chopped

8 tablespoons (1 stick) butter

4 eggs

¼ cup sugar

2 tablespoons vanilla

3 teaspoons cocoa powder

⅛ teaspoon salt

confectioners' sugar, for dusting

Directions

1. Preheat oven to 400°F. Lightly grease 6 ramekins. Dust with white sugar to coat interior and shake out excess. Place on a cookie sheet.

2. In a medium bowl, whisk together all ingredients except chocolate and butter. In a double boiler, melt the chocolate and butter together. Once melted, pour them into the egg mixture and whisk together.

3. Fill the ramekins ¾ of the way full, leaving enough room for the cakes to rise. Bake 10–15 minutes. Check them every 5 minutes or so, and more often near the end. You don't want to overdo it, because then the center won't be molten!

4. Once done, gently invert the ramekin onto a plate and dust with confectioners' sugar. These are great served with ice cream!

Lemon Coconut Petit Fours

MAKES ABOUT 30

Ingredients

CAKE

8 tablespoons (1 stick) salted butter, at room temperature

1 cup sugar

2 eggs

1½ cups sifted all-purpose gluten-free flour

½ cup coconut milk

½ teaspoon pure vanilla extract

LEMON FILLING

1½ cups sugar

1 stick butter

3 eggs

Juice of 1 lemon

Grated rind of 1 lemon

Pinch of salt (optional)

ICING

1 cup confectioners' sugar

3 tablespoons milk

½ teaspoons vanilla

Directions

1. Preheat oven to 350°F. Grease and flour two 9-inch square cake pans.
2. Using an electric mixer, cream butter until fluffy. Add sugar and continue to cream well for 6–8 minutes. Add eggs, one at a time, beating well after each addition. Add flour and milk alternately to creamed mixture, beginning and ending with flour. Add vanilla and continue to beat until just mixed.

continued on next page

3. Spread batter evenly between pans (will be thin). Bake for 12–15 minutes, until cake is golden brown and toothpick inserted comes out clean. Remove and let cool on cooling rack.

4. Meanwhile, make the filling. Mix all ingredients in a saucepan. Boil gently over low heat, stirring continuously, until mixture thickens. Remove from heat and allow to cool.

5. Once cakes and filling are cooled, invert cakes onto a large cutting board or plate. Spread filling over one cake and place the other cake on top. Slice into 1 x 1-inch squares.

6. To make the icing, mix confectioners' sugar, milk, and vanilla together until smooth. (You can use more or less milk depending on how thin you would like the icing to be.) Drizzle icing over squares and serve.

Mini Carrot Cakes

MAKES 48 MINI CUPCAKES

Ingredients

CAKE

½ cup granulated sugar

½ cup brown sugar, packed

4 tablespoons unsalted butter

3 large eggs

1 teaspoon vanilla extract

1½ cups grated carrots

1 (8-ounce) can crushed pineapple, drained

1¼ cups gluten-free all purpose flour

1 teaspoon xanthan gum

1 teaspoon baking powder

½ teaspoon baking soda

½ teaspoon salt

1 teaspoon ground cinnamon

½ teaspoon ground ginger

¼ teaspoon ground cloves

1 cup raisins (optional)

FROSTING

1 (8-ounce) package cream cheese, room temperature

6 tablespoons butter, softened

1 teaspoon vanilla or almond extract

2½ cups confectioners' sugar

GARNISH (optional)

Orange zest

Directions

1. Preheat oven to 350°F. Generously grease 2 (24-cup) mini muffin pans, or line with cupcake liners.

2. In a large mixing bowl, beat together the sugar and butter until fluffy. Add the eggs and vanilla and then the grated carrots and pineapple, beating until combined.

continued on next page

3. In a separate bowl, mix together all the dry ingredients. Add the dry ingredients to the wet ingredients and stir until just combined. Mix in the raisins, if using.

4. Use a teaspoon to fill the muffin cups about ¾ full. Bake for 10–15 minutes, or until edges are lightly browned and a toothpick inserted in the center comes out clean (it should be moist still, but not covered in batter). When done, remove from oven to cool completely before frosting.

5. Meanwhile, make the frosting. In a large mixing bowl, beat together cream cheese, butter, and vanilla or almond extract. Add the confectioners' sugar a little at a time, continuing to beat. Add more if necessary to reach desired consistency.

6. Once cupcakes are cool, scoop frosting into a pastry bag fitted with a star-shaped or wide round tip. Squirt a swirl of frosting on each mini cake. If desired, sprinkle with orange zest.

Mini Gingerbread Pumpkin Cupcakes with Spiced Cream

MAKES 32 CUPCAKES

Ingredients

CUPCAKES

2 cups all-purpose gluten-free flour

2 teaspoons baking powder

2 teaspoons ground ginger

1 teaspoon ground cinnamon

¼ teaspoon salt

1 cup dark brown sugar

½ cup vegetable oil

2 eggs

2 teaspoons vanilla extract

1 cup pumpkin puree

SPICED CREAM

1 cup heavy cream

1 tablespoon honey

½ teaspoon vanilla

¼ teaspoon cinnamon

¼ teaspoon ground ginger

Directions

1. Preheat oven to 350°F. Grease two mini muffin pans and dust with gluten-free flour, or line with cupcake liners.

2. In a large mixing bowl, whisk together the flour, baking powder, ginger, cinnamon, salt, and brown sugar. In a separate bowl, whisk together the oil, eggs, vanilla, and pumpkin. Add the flour mixture to the wet mixture and stir to combine.

3. Fill muffin cups about ¾ full and bake for about 15 minutes, or until a toothpick inserted in the center of a cupcake comes out clean. Remove from oven and allow to cool completely.

continued on next page

4. While cupcakes are cooling, make the spiced cream. In a medium bowl, beat the heavy cream until it becomes light and fluffy. Add the honey, vanilla, cinnamon, and ground ginger, and beat until desired consistency is reached. It should be fairly stiff to hold its shape on the cupcakes. Scoop cream into a pastry bag fitted with a wide round tip. Arrange cupcakes on serving tray and then swirl cream on top of each cupcake.

Mini Chocolate Bundt Cakes with Sour Cream Glaze

MAKES 6 MINI BUNDTS

Ingredients

CAKES

½ cup brewed coffee

½ cup buttermilk (or ½ cup milk mixed with ½ teaspoon vinegar)

½ cup unsalted butter, melted

½ cup cocoa powder, plus more for dusting the pan

1 cup granulated sugar

1 cup gluten-free all-purpose flour

¾ teaspoon baking soda

¼ teaspoon salt

1 egg

½ teaspoon vanilla extract

SOUR CREAM GLAZE

6 ounces bittersweet chocolate, chopped

¾ cup unsalted butter

1 cup confectioners' sugar

½ cup sour cream or Greek-style yogurt

GARNISH (optional)

Fresh berries, crushed nuts, or sifted confectioners' sugar

Directions

1. Preheat oven to 375°F. Brew coffee. Grease the bundt pans and generously sift cocoa powder over them to prevent the cakes from sticking after they're baked.

2. In a large bowl, whisk together the melted coffee, buttermilk, butter, and cocoa powder. Add the sugar and whisk until dissolved. In a separate bowl, whisk together the flour, baking soda, and salt.

continued on next page

3. Allow butter mixture to cool if it's still hot from the brewed coffee. Whisk in the egg and vanilla. Add the dry ingredients and mix until combined. Divide mixture between 6 mini bundt cups and bake 20–25 minutes, or until a toothpick inserted into one comes out clean. Remove from oven and allow to cool completely before removing from pans.

4. Meanwhile, prepare the glaze. In a double boiler, melt the chocolate pieces, stirring constantly. Add the butter and continue stirring until incorporated. Gradually add the confectioners' sugar, and then the sour cream. Whisk until glossy.

5. Carefully remove the bundt cakes from the pan and place on large cutting board or other work surface. Drizzle the glaze over the cakes and then allow to sit until glaze sets. Garnish as desired.

Cranberry Pound Cake with Lemon Glaze

MAKES 12 CAKES

Ingredients

CAKES

Confectioners' sugar (for dusting pans)

1 cup butter, unsalted

1¼ cups brown sugar

3 eggs

1 teaspoon vanilla

1½ cups gluten-free all-purpose flour

1½ teaspoons baking powder

½ teaspoon salt

2 cups cranberries

LEMON GLAZE

2 cups confectioners' sugar

2 tablespoons milk

2 teaspoons lemon juice

Directions

1. Preheat oven to 350°F. Grease six bundt pans and generously dust with confectioners' sugar to prevent the cakes from sticking after they're baked.

2. In a medium mixing bowl, beat together the butter and brown sugar. Add the eggs, one at a time, while beating, and then add the vanilla.

3. In a separate bowl, whisk together the flour, baking powder, and salt. Add the flour mixture to the wet mixture, stirring to combine. Fold in the cranberries and then divide batter between bundt

continued on next page

pans and bake 20–25 minutes, or until a toothpick inserted in one comes out clean. Remove from oven and allow to cool completely before removing from pans.

4. Meanwhile, prepare the glaze. Mix together confectioners' sugar and milk until smooth. Add lemon juice and whisk.

5. Carefully remove the bundt cakes from the pan and place on large cutting board or other work surface. Drizzle the glaze over the cakes and then allow to sit until glaze sets.

Lemon Poundcake with Fruit and Cream

Ingredients

CAKES

Confectioners' sugar (for dusting
    pans)
1 cup butter, unsalted
1¼ cups brown sugar
3 eggs
1½ teaspoons lemon juice
1 teaspoon lemon zest

1 teaspoon almond extract
1½ cups gluten-free all purpose
    flour
1½ teaspoons baking powder
½ teaspoon salt
2 cups cranberries

LEMON GLAZE

2 cups confectioners' sugar
2 tablespoons milk

2 teaspoons lemon juice

GARNISH

Fresh berries or your favorite fruit

Whipped cream

Directions

1. Preheat oven to 350°F. Grease six bundt pans and generously dust with confectioners' sugar to prevent the cakes from sticking after they're baked.

2. In a medium mixing bowl, beat together the butter and brown sugar. Add the eggs, one at a time, while beating, and then add the lemon juice, lemon zest, and almond extract.

3. In a separate bowl, whisk together the flour, baking powder, and salt. Add the flour mixture to the wet mixture, stirring to combine. Fold in the cranberries and then divide batter between pans and bake 20–25 minutes, or until a toothpick inserted in one comes

out clean. Remove from oven and allow to cool completely before removing from pans.

4. Meanwhile, prepare the glaze. Mix together confectioners' sugar and milk until smooth. Add lemon juice and whisk.

5. Carefully remove the bundt cakes from the pan and place on large cutting board or other work surface. Drizzle the glaze over the cakes and allow to sit until glaze sets. Garnish with fresh fruit and add a dollop of whipped cream just before serving.

Almond Bundt Cake with Chocolate Glaze

MAKES 12 CAKES

Ingredients

CAKES

Confectioners' sugar (for dusting pans)

1 cup butter, unsalted

1¼ cups brown sugar

3 eggs

CHOCOLATE GLAZE

6 ounces bittersweet chocolate, chopped

¾ cup unsalted butter

2 teaspoons almond extract

1 cup gluten-free all purpose flour

½ cup almond meal

1½ teaspoons baking powder

½ teaspoon salt

1 cup confectioners' sugar

Sliced almonds, for garnish

Directions

1. Preheat oven to 350°F. Grease six bundt pans and generously dust with confectioners' sugar to prevent the cakes from sticking after they're baked.

2. In a medium mixing bowl, beat together the butter and brown sugar. Add the eggs, one at a time, while beating, and then add the almond extract.

3. In a separate bowl, whisk together the flour, almond meal, baking powder, and salt. Add the flour mixture to the wet mixture, stirring to combine. Divide batter between pans and bake 20–25 minutes, or until a toothpick inserted in one comes out clean. Remove from oven and allow to cool completely before removing from pans.

4. Meanwhile, prepare the glaze. In a double boiler, melt the chocolate pieces, stirring constantly. Add the butter and continue

stirring until incorporated. Gradually add the confectioners' sugar. Whisk until glossy.

5. Carefully remove the bundt cakes from the pan and place on large cutting board or other work surface. Drizzle the glaze over the cakes and then allow to sit until glaze sets. Garnish with sliced almonds.

{ Pies, Crisps, and Tartlets }

Ginger Cream Tartlets	30
Lemon-Blueberry Tartlets	32
Chocolate-Raspberry Ganache Tartlets	34
Cherry Mascarpone Tartlets	36
Classic Whoopie Pies	38
Pumpkin Whoopie Pies with Maple Cream Filling	40
Pop Tarts	42
Apple Crumb Cups	44
Raspberry Peach Cobbler	46
Caramelized Pear Pies	49
Strawberry Rhubarb Pies	50
Mocha Souffles	51
Tollhouse Cookie Pies	53
Rhubarb Shortcake Sliders	54
Mini Apple Turnovers	57
Cherry Clafoutis	58
Rustic Plum Galettes	60
Simple Jam Galettes	62
Empanaditas	64

Ginger Cream Tartlets

MAKES ABOUT 2 DOZEN TARTLETS

Ingredients

SHELLS

1 cup all-purpose gluten-free flour

½ cup almond meal

½ teaspoon xanthan gum

¼ cup sugar

¼ teaspoon salt

4 tablespoons butter, melted

1 teaspoon vanilla

3 tablespoons milk

FILLING

1 (8-ounce) package cream cheese

½ cup heavy cream

½ teaspoon almond extract

2 tablespoons confectioners' sugar

¼ cup crystallized ginger, finely chopped

Directions

1. Preheat oven to 350°F. Generously grease a mini tart tin with cooking spray or butter.

2. In a large mixing bowl, whisk together the flour, almond meal, xanthan gum, sugar, and salt. Add the melted butter, vanilla, and milk, and mix. Use your hands to knead the dough until it hangs together and becomes smooth.

3. Take a small chunk of dough, roll it into a ball between your palms, and place it in one of the tart cups. Use a pestle (from a mortar and pestle) to press the dough down so that it spreads up the sides of the cup. Repeat until all cups are filled.

4. Place mini tart tin in the oven and bake for about 10 minutes or until the shells are slightly golden. Remove from oven, press the dough down again if it has puffed up, and allow to cool.

5. In a large mixing bowl, beat together the cream cheese, heavy cream, almond extract, and confectioners' sugar until creamy. Put a heaping teaspoon of filling into the bottom of each tart shell. Sprinkle crystallized ginger on top. These are best served immediately, but leftovers can be stored in the refrigerator for up to 3 days.

Lemon-Blueberry Tartlets

Ingredients

SHELLS

1 cup all-purpose gluten-free flour

½ cup almond meal

½ teaspoon xanthan gum

¼ cup sugar

¼ teaspoon salt

4 tablespoons butter, melted

1 teaspoon vanilla

3 tablespoons milk

FILLING

1 (8-ounce) package cream cheese

½ cup sugar

2 large eggs plus 2 yolks

½ cup fresh squeezed lemon juice

1 tablespoon lemon zest

2 cups fresh blueberries, rinsed and drained

Directions

1. Preheat oven to 350°F. Generously grease a mini tart tin with cooking spray or butter.

2. In a large mixing bowl, whisk together the flour, almond meal, xanthan gum, sugar, and salt. Add the melted butter, vanilla, and milk and mix. Use your hands to knead the dough until it hangs together and becomes smooth.

3. Take a small chunk of dough, roll it into a ball between your palms, and place it in one of the tart cups. Use a pestle (from a mortar and pestle) to press the dough down so that it spreads up the sides of the cup. Repeat until all cups are filled.

4. Place mini tart tin in the oven and bake for about 5 minutes or until the shells are slightly golden. Remove from oven and press the dough down again if it has puffed up.

5. In a large mixing bowl, beat together the cream cheese and sugar. Add the eggs, one at a time, beating until smooth. Finally add the lemon juice and lemon zest.

6. Fill each tart shell to pan level and return to oven to bake for about 10 minutes, or until filling is set. Remove from oven and allow to cool. Sprinkle tarts with the crystallized ginger and serve. Leftovers can be stored in the refrigerator for up to 3 days.

Chocolate-Raspberry Ganache Tartlets

MAKES ABOUT 2 DOZEN TARTLETS

Ingredients

SHELLS

1 cup all-purpose gluten-free flour

½ cup almond meal

½ teaspoon xanthan gum

¼ cup sugar

¼ teaspoon salt

4 tablespoons butter, melted

1 teaspoon vanilla

3 tablespoons milk

GANACHE

8 ounces bittersweet chocolate, chopped

1 cup heavy cream

4 tablespoons butter, softened

½ cup raspberry preserves

1 pint fresh raspberries, for garnish

Directions

1. Preheat oven to 350°F. Generously grease a mini tart tin with cooking spray or butter.

2. In a large mixing bowl, whisk together the flour, almond meal, xanthan gum, sugar, and salt. Add the melted butter, vanilla, and milk, and mix. Use your hands to knead the dough until it hangs together and becomes smooth.

3. Take a small chunk of dough, roll it into a ball between your palms, and place it in one of the tart cups. Use a pestle (from a mortar and pestle) to press the dough down so that it spreads up the sides of the cup. Repeat until all cups are filled.

4. Place mini tart tin in the oven and bake for about 10 minutes or until the shells are slightly golden. Remove from oven, press the dough down again if it has puffed up, and allow to cool.

5. To make the ganache, place chocolate bits in a medium bowl. In a saucepan, heat heavy cream to a simmer. Remove from heat and pour over chocolate bits. Add preserves and use a whisk to stir in slow circles until combined. Add butter, 1 tablespoon at a time, continuing to mix slowly until ganache is smooth and thick.

6. Divide ganache between tartlet shells, using a teaspoon or piping it in with a pastry bag. Garnish with a single fresh raspberry on top. Serve immediately, or refrigerate for up to 3 days.

Cherry Mascarpone Tartlets

Ingredients

SHELLS

1 cup all-purpose gluten-free flour

½ cup almond meal

½ teaspoon xanthan gum

¼ cup sugar

¼ teaspoon salt

4 tablespoons butter, melted

1 teaspoon vanilla

3 tablespoons milk

FILLING

1 cup mascarpone cheese

½ cup pitted cherries, crushed into small pieces

1 teaspoon almond extract

1 tablespoon honey

1 cup toasted almonds, chopped, or pistachios

Directions

1. Preheat oven to 350°F. Generously grease a mini tart tin with cooking spray or butter. In a large mixing bowl, whisk together the flour, almond meal, xanthan gum, sugar, and salt. Add the melted butter, vanilla, and milk, and mix. Use your hands to knead the dough until it hangs together and becomes smooth.

2. Take a small chunk of dough, roll it into a ball between your palms, and place it in one of the tart cups. Use a pestle (from a mortar and pestle) to press the dough down so that it spreads up the sides of the cup. Repeat until all cups are filled.

3. Place mini tart tin in the oven and bake for about 10 minutes or until the shells are slightly golden. Remove from oven, press the dough down again if it has puffed up, and allow to cool.

4. In a medium bowl, mix together mascarpone cheese, cherries, almond extract, and honey. Fill each tartlet shell with the mixture and garnish with the toasted almonds or pistachios.

Classic Whoopie Pies

MAKES ABOUT 16 SMALL WHOOPIE PIES

Ingredients

CAKE

½ cup Dutch process cocoa powder

2½ cups all-purpose gluten-free flour

1 teaspoon baking powder

1 teaspoon baking soda

½ teaspoon salt

1 stick unsalted butter, room temperature

1 cup sugar

1 large egg, room temperature

1 teaspoon vanilla extract

1 cup buttermilk (if you don't have buttermilk, you can make your own by mixing 1 cup of milk with 3½ teaspoons of lemon juice or white vinegar)

FILLING

½ cup (1 stick) unsalted butter

½ cup marshmallow fluff

¾ cup confectioners' sugar

1 teaspoon vanilla extract

Directions

1. Preheat oven to 350°F. Line two baking sheets with parchment paper or silicone baking mats and set aside.

2. Sift cocoa powder, flour, baking powder, baking soda, and salt into a large bowl. In a separate bowl, beat together butter and sugar until fluffy. Add egg and vanilla and mix until all are combined.

3. In separate bowl, combine half the flour with the butter mixture and mix well. Slowly add in buttermilk and continue mixing. When mixture is consistent, add remaining flour and mix until smooth.

4. Scoop heaping tablespoons of batter onto the prepared pans. Allow about 2 inches of space between each as cakes will spread as they bake.

5. Bake on center rack for 15–18 minutes, until a toothpick inserted comes out clean and the cakes spring back when touched. Remove from oven and immediately transfer cakes and parchment paper onto a cooling rack to cool completely.

6. To prepare the filling, beat together the butter, fluff, and sugar. Slowly add ¾ cup confectioners' sugar and continue beating. Add 1 teaspoon vanilla extract and mix so all ingredients are thoroughly combined.

7. Transfer the filling to a pastry bag with a round tip. Pipe a dollop of filling on the flat side of half of the cooled cakes. Sandwich with remaining cookies.

VARIATIONS

Add orange, lemon, or mint extracts instead of vanilla to give the cream filling a zing!

Pumpkin Whoopie Pies with Maple Cream Filling

MAKES ABOUT 16 SMALL WHOOPIE PIES

Ingredients

CAKE

3 cups all-purpose gluten-free flour

½ teaspoon salt

1 teaspoon baking powder

1 teaspoon baking soda

1 teaspoon cinnamon

½ teaspoon ground cloves

1 stick (½ cup) unsalted butter,
  room temperature

1 cup brown sugar, firmly packed

2 large eggs, room temperature

1 teaspoon vanilla extract

2½ cups pumpkin puree

1 tablespoon molasses

FILLING

1 stick (½ cup) unsalted butter,
  softened

1 (8-ounce) package cream cheese,
  softened

¼ cup pure maple syrup

1 teaspoon maple extract (optional)

3 cups confectioners' sugar

Directions

1. Preheat oven to 350°F with tray on middle oven rack. Line two baking sheets with parchment paper or silicone baking mats and set aside.

2. Sift flour, salt, baking powder, baking soda, cinnamon, and cloves into a large bowl. In a separate bowl, beat together butter and brown sugar until fluffy. Add eggs, vanilla, pumpkin puree, and molasses and mix until all are combined.

3. In separate bowl, combine half the flour with the butter mixture and mix well. Add remaining flour and mix until smooth.

4. Scoop heaping tablespoons of batter onto the prepared pans. Allow about 2 inches of space between each as cakes will spread as they bake.

5. Bake on center rack for 15–18 minutes, until a toothpick inserted comes out clean and the cakes spring back when touched. Remove from oven and immediately transfer cakes and parchment paper onto a cooling rack to cool completely.

6. To prepare the filling, beat together the butter, cream cheese, maple syrup, and maple extract if using. Gradually add the confectioners' sugar and continue beating.

7. Transfer the filling to a pastry bag with a round tip. Pipe a dollop of filling on the flat side of half of the cooled cakes. Sandwich with remaining cookies.

Pop Tarts

Ingredients

PASTRY

1½ cups all-purpose gluten-free flour

½ teaspoon xanthan gum

¼ cup sugar

FILLING

6 tablespoons jam

¼ teaspoon salt

4 tablespoons butter, melted

1 teaspoon vanilla

3 tablespoons milk

Directions

1. Preheat oven to 350°F. Line a baking sheet with parchment paper.
2. In a large mixing bowl, whisk together the flour, xanthan gum, sugar, and salt. Add the melted butter, vanilla, and milk and mix. Use your hands to knead the dough until it hangs together and becomes smooth.
3. Line a flat work surface with parchment paper and dust with gluten-free flour. Turn the dough onto the surface and place another piece of parchment paper over top. Roll out the dough to about ¼-inch thick. Peel away the top piece of parchment paper and slice dough into squares, hearts, or circles. Gather scraps into a ball, roll out again, and repeat until dough is all used up.
4. Spoon a little jam into the center of the pastry. Place another pastry cut-out on top. Use the back of a fork to seal the edges. Transfer to a lightly greased baking sheet and bake for 8–10 minutes, or until the edges begin to turn golden. Transfer to wire rack to cool.

Apple Crumb Cups

MAKES 8–10 SERVINGS

Ingredients

8 medium apples, peeled and sliced

¾ cup gluten-free oats

¾ cup all-purpose gluten-free flour

1 cup brown sugar

1 teaspoon cinnamon

½ teaspoon nutmeg

1 stick (½ cup) butter, cut into pieces

Whipped cream

Directions

1. Preheat oven to 350°F.
2. Divide apple slices between 8–10 ramekins. In a medium mixing bowl, combine oats, flour, brown sugar, cinnamon, and nutmeg. Mix the butter in, using two forks, a pastry cutter, or your fingers to incorporate.
3. Place ramekins on a cookie sheet and divide topping between them. Bake for 35–40 minutes, or until topping is golden and bubbly. Cool before serving so that ramekins don't burn your fingers. Serve with whipped cream.

VARIATION

Rather than baking in ramekins, you can bake in a 2-quart casserole dish and then scoop into tea cups or shot glasses to serve.

Raspberry Peach Cobbler

MAKES 8–10 SERVINGS

Ingredients

5 medium peaches, peeled and
sliced
2 cups fresh or frozen raspberries
1 tablespoon cornstarch
¾ cup gluten-free oats
¾ cup all-purpose gluten-free flour

1 cup brown sugar
1 teaspoon cinnamon
½ teaspoon nutmeg
1 stick (½ cup) butter, cut into
pieces

Directions

1. Preheat oven to 350°F.
2. In a large bowl, mix together peach slices, raspberries, and corn-starch. Divide between 8–10 ramekins. In a medium mixing bowl, combine oats, flour, brown sugar, cinnamon, and nutmeg. Mix the butter in, using two forks, a pastry cutter, or your fingers to incorporate.
3. Place ramekins on a cookie sheet and divide topping between them. Bake for 35–40 minutes, or until topping is golden and bubbly. Cool before serving so that ramekins don't burn your fingers.

VARIATION

Rather than baking in ramekins, you can bake in a 2-quart casserole dish and then scoop into tea cups to serve.

GLUTEN-FREE PIECRUST

Ingredients

1 cup white rice flour

¼ cup potato starch (not potato flour)

¼ cup tapioca starch

1 teaspoon xanthan gum

1 teaspoon salt

2 tablespoons sugar

½ cup butter, cold

2 to 4 tablespoons ice water

Directions

Combine all dry ingredients in a food processor fitted with a steel blade and pulse to mix. Cut butter into ½ inch pieces, add to flour mixture, and pulse until mixture forms a coarse meal. Add ice water a little at a time, pulsing until dough begins to hold together.

Remove the dough from the food processor and form into a ball. Flatten it slightly, wrap in plastic wrap, and refrigerate for at least one hour. Remove from refrigerator a few minutes before ready to use. Roll the dough between two pieces of waxed paper sprinkled with gluten-free flour.

Note: to make chocolate pastry, add 2 tablespoons of cocoa powder to the dry ingredients and increase the sugar to 3 tablespoons.

Caramelized Pear Pies

Ingredients

Pastry for 4 top and bottom crusts (see page 48)

3 tablespoons brown sugar

2 tablespoons cornstarch

1 teaspoon cinnamon

⅛ teaspoon salt

½ teaspoon lemon zest (optional)

1 (15.25-ounce) can pears in fruit juice (not syrup)

1 tablespoon butter

Directions

1. Preheat oven to 400°F.
2. In a medium bowl, combine brown sugar, cornstarch, cinnamon, salt, and lemon zest (if using).
3. Drain pears, slice, and add to brown sugar mixture. Toss to coat pears.
4. Line muffin tins (or a mini pie maker appliance) with bottom piecrusts for 4 pies. Divide pears between the four pies. Dot each pie with pats of butter. Cover with top crusts and bake for 15–17 minutes (or in a mini pie maker for 10 to 12 minutes) or until the crusts are golden.

Strawberry Rhubarb Pies

Ingredients

Pastry for 4 top and bottom crusts
  (see page 48)
2 cups chopped rhubarb

1 cup granulated sugar
1 cup strawberries, hulled and sliced
1 tablespoon butter

Directions

1. Preheat oven to 400°F. Line muffin tins (or a mini pie maker appliance) with bottom piecrusts for 4 pies.
2. In a saucepan, heat rhubarb and sugar and simmer for about 10 minutes, or until the rhubarb starts to become soft. Add strawberries and simmer for another 3–4 minutes. Add butter and mix until melted and combined. Remove from heat.
3. Divide filling between crusts. Slice top pastry rounds into strips to create a lattice top over each pie.
4. Bake in the oven for 12–15 minutes (or in a mini pie maker for 8–10 minutes), or until the crusts are golden.

Mocha Souffles

Ingredients

Pastry for 4 bottom crusts
(see page 48)

2 eggs

5 ounces bittersweet chocolate,
chopped

1 tablespoon butter

½ cup sugar

2 tablespoons instant coffee
granules

Whipped cream for serving

Directions

1. Preheat oven to 400°F. Line muffin tins (or a mini pie maker appliance) with bottom piecrusts for 4 pies.

2. Beat eggs until light and fluffy.

3. In a double boiler, melt chocolate and butter. Add sugar and coffee and mix. Remove from heat and fold in beaten eggs.

4. Use a ladle to divide filling between crusts. Bake in the oven for 12–15 minutes (or in a mini pie maker for 8–10 minutes), or until the crusts are golden.

5. Serve with a dollop of whipped cream over each pie.

Tollhouse Cookie Pies

Ingredients

Chocolate pastry for 4 bottom crusts (see page 48)

⅔ cup brown sugar

¼ cup gluten-free all-purpose flour

2 eggs, lightly beaten

3 tablespoons butter, melted

1 teaspoon vanilla extract

1 cup peanuts, walnuts, or pecans, crushed

¾ cup chocolate chips

Directions

1. Preheat oven to 400°F. Line muffin tins (or a mini pie maker appliance) with bottom piecrusts for 4 pies.

2. Combine brown sugar, flour, eggs, butter, and vanilla. Add nuts and chocolate chips and mix.

3. Divide filling between crusts. Bake in the oven for 12–15 minutes (or in a mini pie maker for 8–10 minutes), or until the crusts are golden and filling is set.

Rhubarb Shortcake Sliders

Ingredients

BISCUITS

2½ cups gluten-free all-purpose
 flour

2 tablespoons granulated sugar

1 tablespoon baking powder

½ teaspoon salt

½ cup (1 stick) cold, unsalted butter,
 cut into small cubes

1 cup heavy whipping cream

1 large egg

1 teaspoon vanilla extract

FILLING

4 stalks fresh rhubarb, sliced in
 ½-inch pieces

⅓ cup granulated sugar

WHIPPED CREAM

1 cup heavy whipping cream

1 tablespoon granulated sugar

½ teaspoon vanilla

Directions

1. Preheat oven to 425°F. Grease a baking sheet.

2. In a large bowl, whisk together the flour, sugar, salt, and baking powder. Cut the butter into small cubes and add to the flour mixture. Mix until the largest pieces of butter are the size of peas.

3. In a separate bowl, whisk together the cream, egg, and vanilla. Make a well in the flour mixture and pour the cream mixture into the center of it. Use a fork to stir until the dough is evenly mixed. Knead the dough with your hands eight turns or so to create a ball.

4. Lightly flour a cutting board with gluten-free flour and roll the dough out until it is between ¼ and ½-inch thick. Use a small (1½-inch diameter or so) round cookie cutter or the top of a shot glass

continued on page 56

to cut the dough into rounds. Place rounds on greased baking sheet, spaced about 1½ to 2 inches apart. Chill for 10 minutes in the refrigerator before baking.

5. Bake biscuits on middle rack for 12 minutes, or until risen and lightly browned. Remove from oven and let cool.

6. Meanwhile, put the rhubarb and sugar in a saucepan with about ½ cup water and simmer until rhubarb becomes soft.

7. Beat the cream until it becomes light and fluffy. Sprinkle the sugar and vanilla over the cream. Continue to whip until it is thick and holds its shape. Cover with plastic wrap and keep chilled until it's time to assemble the shortcakes.

8. To assemble, place a spoonful of rhubarb on the bottom of one shortcake, followed by a dollop of whipped cream. Place the top biscuit piece on top and repeat until biscuits are all used.

Mini Apple Turnovers

MAKES ABOUT A DOZEN TURNOVERS

Ingredients

PASTRY

1½ cups all-purpose gluten-free
   flour

½ teaspoon xanthan gum

¼ cup sugar

¼ teaspoon salt

4 tablespoons butter, melted

1 teaspoon vanilla

3 tablespoons milk

FILLING

5 medium apples, peeled and sliced

2 tablespoons butter, divided

¾ cup sugar

2 teaspoons cinnamon

Directions

1. Preheat oven to 375°F. Generously grease a baking sheet. In a large bowl, whisk together the flour, xanthan gum, sugar, and salt. Add the melted butter, vanilla, and milk and mix. Use your hands to knead the dough until it hangs together and becomes smooth.

2. Line a flat work surface with parchment paper and dust with gluten-free flour. Turn the dough onto the surface and place another piece of parchment paper over top. Roll out the dough to about ¼-inch thick. Peel away the top piece of parchment paper and slice dough into squares about 4 inches across. Gather scraps into a ball, roll out again, and repeat until dough is all used up.

3. In a large skillet, sauté the apple pieces with the butter, sugar, and cinnamon until apples become soft. Place about 1½ teaspoons of apple filling in one corner of each pastry square. Fold the pastry over to form a triangle, and seal the edges. Place on baking sheet, prick with a fork, and repeat until filling is all used. Bake for 18–22 minutes, or until golden. Remove from oven and allow to cool on a wire rack for several minutes before serving.

Cherry Clafoutis

Ingredients

4 eggs

¾ cup sugar

2 teaspoons lemon zest

1 teaspoon vanilla

1 cup milk (cow's milk, coconut milk, or almond milk)

¾ cup gluten-free all purpose flour or almond flour

¼ teaspoon salt

1 cup halved and pitted cherries

Confectioners' sugar, for dusting.

Directions

1. Preheat oven to 325°F. Grease 24 mini muffin cups.

2. In a large mixing bowl, beat together eggs, sugar, lemon zest, and vanilla. Add milk, and beat another 30 seconds or so. Stir in the flour and salt.

3. Fill each muffin cup about ¾ of the way, place 3 or 4 cherry halves on top of the batter in each cup, and bake for 20–25 minutes, or until a toothpick inserted in the middle of one comes out clean. Just before serving, dust with confectioners' sugar.

Rustic Plum Galettes

Ingredients

PASTRY

1½ cups gluten-free all purpose flour

½ cup almond flour

¼ teaspoon salt

2 tablespoons sugar

½ cup (1 stick) butter, cut into tablespoons

6–8 tablespoons ice water

Turbinado sugar, for sprinkling

PLUM FILLING

½ cup sugar

3 tablespoons ground almonds

1 tablespoon cornstarch

½ cup plum, apricot, or raspberry preserves

3 tablespoons unsalted butter

2 pounds fresh plums, pitted and sliced into thin wedges

Directions

1. In a food processor, combine flour, almond flour, salt, and sugar and pulse to mix. Add the butter and pulse until coarse crumbs form. Add 4 tablespoons water, pulse, and then add 1 tablespoon at a time until dough hangs together. Place a large piece of parchment paper on a flat work surface, form dough into a ball, and place the ball on top of the paper. Cover with another large piece of parchment paper and roll out to about ⅛-inch thick. Refrigerate for about 20 minutes.

2. Mix together the sugar, ground almonds, cornstarch, and preserves in a small mixing bowl.

3. When the dough is chilled, preheat oven to 375°F. Cut the dough into circles about 4 inches in diameter and arrange on a baking sheet. Gather dough scraps and repeat.

4. Spread the dough rounds with the filling mixture, leaving a 1 inch border. Dot with butter, and then arrange a few plum slices on each one. Fold up the pastry edges, pressing lightly to adhere as necessary. Sprinkle the edges with turbinado sugar.

5. Bake for 40–45 minutes, or until pastry is golden. Remove from oven and cool on wire racks.

Pies, Crisps, and Tartlets　{ 61 }

Simple Jam Galettes

MAKES ABOUT 10

Ingredients

PASTRY

1½ cups gluten-free all purpose flour

½ cup almond flour

¼ teaspoon salt

2 tablespoons sugar

½ cup (1 stick) butter, cut into table-spoons

6–8 tablespoons ice water

Turbinado sugar, for sprinkling

FILLING

1 cup jam or preserves, any variety

Directions

1. In a food processor, combine flour, almond flour, salt, and sugar and pulse to mix. Add the butter and pulse until coarse crumbs form. Add 4 tablespoons water, pulse, and then add 1 tablespoon at a time until dough hangs together. Place a large piece of parchment paper on a flat work surface, form dough into a ball, and place the ball on top of the paper. Cover with another large piece of parchment paper and roll out to about ⅛-inch thick. Refrigerate for about 20 minutes.

2. When the dough is chilled, preheat oven to 375°F. Cut the dough into circles about 4 inches in diameter and arrange on a baking sheet. Gather dough scraps and repeat.

3. Spread the dough rounds with the jam, leaving a 1-inch border. Fold up the pastry edges, pressing lightly to adhere as necessary. Sprinkle the edges with turbinado sugar.

4. Bake for 40–45 minutes, or until pastry is golden. Remove from oven and cool on wire racks.

Empanaditas

MAKES ABOUT 10

Ingredients

1 cup unsalted butter, softened

1 (8-ounce) package cream cheese, softened

1½ cup gluten-free all-purpose flour

½ cup cornmeal

1 cup dulce de leche (or Nutella)

2 medium bananas

Cinnamon sugar for sprinkling

Directions

1. In a medium mixing bowl, beat together the butter and cream cheese. Gradually add the flour, beating at low speed, until all the flour is incorporated. Gather the dough into two balls, wrap each in plastic wrap, and refrigerate for at least 2 hours.

2. Heat oven to 375°F and grease a baking sheet. Place a large sheet of waxed paper on a flat work surface, place one ball of dough in the center, and lay a second sheet of waxed paper over the top. Roll out the dough to about ⅛-inch thick.

3. Cut dough into 3 x 3-inch squares. Spread a little dulce de leche on half the squares and place a few thin slices of banana on top. Cover with another pastry square and use a fork to seal the edges. Sprinkle with cinnamon sugar

4. Bake for 12–15 minutes or until golden.

Mousses, Puddings, and Parfaits

Maple Crême Brûlée	68
Cream Puffs	69
Coconut Key Lime Shooters	71
Tiramisu Cups	74
Peanut Butter Mousse in Chocolate Cups	75
Lemon Mousse in White Chocolate Cups	78
Coconut Rice Pudding with Custard Sauce	79
Chocolate Espresso Pots de Crème	81
Blueberry Trifle	82
Festive Fruit Parfaits	84

Maple Crème Brûlée

Ingredients

8 egg yolks

6 tablespoons real maple syrup
(grade B works best)

2 teaspoons vanilla

2 cups minus 2 tablespoons heavy
cream

Sugar (about 2 teaspoons, for
dusting)

Directions

1. Preheat oven to 300°F.
2. In a bowl, whisk together 8 yolks with syrup until thoroughly blended. Add vanilla and cream. Whisk again to blend. After whisking, you may want to strain as heavy cream sometimes leaves lumps in mixture.
3. Fill 4 standard ramekins to top. Place ramekins in cake pan (may need two) or any oven safe tray with high sides. Slowly fill with warm water to just below tops of the ramekins.
4. Bake 50–60 minutes, or until edges are firm and the center is still a little wiggly. Carefully remove from oven and chill at least 2 hours in refrigerator.
5. Once cooled, sprinkle sugar on the custard to coat. Use torch to caramelize sugar. If you don't have a torch, you can broil on high for about two minutes, until sugar melts and browns. Let cool thoroughly before serving. Serve in the ramekins.

VARIATION

Sprinkle chocolate chips in bottom of ramekins before adding custard for a delicious chocolate "crust."

Cream Puffs

MAKES ABOUT 16-18 PUFFS, DEPENDING ON SIZE

Ingredients

PUFFS

1 cup water	½ teaspoon salt
2 sticks butter	2 teaspoons sugar
1 cup gluten-free all purpose flour	4 eggs

CUSTARD FILLING

2 cups milk	6 large egg yolks
½ cup sugar	2 tablespoons vanilla
6 tablespoons all-purpose gluten-free flour	

Directions

1. Preheat oven to 425°F and lightly grease a cookie sheet.
2. Combine water and butter in saucepan and bring to a boil. Meanwhile, in a mixing bowl, combine flour, salt, and sugar. When the water and butter mixture begins to boil, remove from heat and add the flour mixture. Mix until dough ball forms. Allow to cool for 5 minutes.
3. Once cool, add eggs one at a time and mix thoroughly. Drop tablespoon-sized dollops onto cookie sheet (amount and size can vary depending on how big you want the puffs). Bake until puffs are golden brown and firm (10–15 minutes, again depending on size). Remove from oven and place on cooling rack (if you wish, carefully prick tops with toothpick to allow steam to escape).

continued on next page

4. Meanwhile, make the custard filling. In a saucepan, bring the milk to a boil with ¼ cup of sugar. Whisk the egg yolks in a separate bowl with the salt and remaining sugar. Sift the flour over the egg mixture and whisk it in until smooth. When the milk boils, slowly whisk ⅓ of it into the egg mixture. Then slowly add the egg mixture to the milk in the saucepan. You must follow these steps to gradually raise the temperature of the eggs. If you add them all at once to the hot milk, they will curdle.

5. Return the saucepan to a medium heat and again bring to a boil, whisking continually. The mixture should begin to thicken. Allow it to boil for another minute. Remove from heat and whisk in the vanilla and cinnamon. Transfer the pastry cream to a bowl. Cover with plastic wrap and refrigerate until very cold, about 2 hours.

6. Just before serving, fill the puffs. Use a sharp knife to slice off the puff tops. Fill with custard, and serve immediately.

VARIATIONS

Try adding some zest of orange or lemon to the milk and sugar before boiling. Or for chocolate, stir in ¾ cup chocolate chips to hot custard as it comes off of the heat. Whisk smooth as it cools off.

For a simpler variation, you can also fill the puffs with whipped cream or jam, or a combination.

Coconut Key Lime Shooters

Ingredients

BOTTOM LAYER

1½ cups crushed gluten-free
graham crackers (9–10 crackers)

4 tablespoons butter, melted

MIDDLE LAYER

1 (8-ounce) package cream cheese,
room temperature

1 can (14 ounces) sweetened
condensed milk

1 tablespoon lime zest

⅓ cup lime juice

TOP LAYER

1 pint heavy cream

2 tablespoons sugar

½ teaspoon vanilla

½ cup coconut flakes, lightly
toasted, divided

Directions

1. In a medium mixing bowl, combine the graham cracker crumbs with the butter and mix until dough hangs together. Divide between six 3-ounce shot glasses.

2. To make the filling, beat together the cream cheese and sweetened condensed milk. Add the lime zest and lime juice and beat until incorporated. Divide between the shot glasses.

continued on next page

3. For the topping, beat the cream until light and fluffy. Add the sugar and vanilla and beat until desired consistency is reached. Fold in ¼ cup toasted coconut flakes. Divide between shot glasses. Top with remaining ¼ cup toasted coconut flakes.

Tiramisu Cups

Ingredients

BOTTOM LAYER

¾ cup brewed espresso or strong
   coffee

1 tablespoon rum
12 gluten-free lady finger cookies

TOP LAYER

2 cups mascarpone cheese
½ cup sugar

1 cup heavy cream

GARNISH

Cocoa powder and/or chocolate
   shavings

Directions

1. In a bowl, combine the espresso and rum. Dip the lady fingers in the bowl and then break into small pieces and divide between 8 tea cups, ramekins, or shot glasses.

2. To make the topping, beat together the mascarpone and sugar. In a separate bowl, beat the heavy cream until light and fluffy. Fold the whipped cream into the mascarpone and sugar mixture. Layer on top of the cookies. Garnish with cocoa powder and/or chocolate shavings arranged on top.

Peanut Butter Mousse in Chocolate Cups

MAKES 24

Ingredients

CHOCOLATE CUPS

24 foil candy cup liners

16 ounces chocolate chips

MOUSSE

1 (8-ounce) package cream cheese

½ cup creamy peanut butter

½ cup confectioners' sugar

1 teaspoon vanilla

½ cup heavy cream

GARNISH (optional)

Chocolate shavings

Directions

1. In a double boiler over low heat, melt the chocolate. Use a clean paint brush (preferably one that has never been used for paint) to paint the inside of one candy cup liner with chocolate. Paint the bottom and inside edges generously and then place on a cookie sheet. Work quickly and repeat until all the chocolate is used up. Place pan in the freezer.

2. To make the mousse, beat together the cream cheese, peanut butter, sugar, and vanilla until smooth. In a separate bowl, beat the heavy cream until light and fluffy. Fold half of it into the peanut butter mixture, and then fold in the other half (this will help keep it light). Fold gently until mixture is smooth. Cover and refrigerate for at least 2 hours.

continued on next page

3. Remove the chocolate cups from the freezer and carefully peel away the foil liners. Scoop the peanut butter mousse into the chocolate cups with a spoon, or fill a pastry bag fitted with a large star tip and pipe a generous swirl into each chocolate cup. Garnish with chocolate shavings, if desired.

Lemon Mousse in White Chocolate Cups

MAKES 24

Ingredients

WHITE CHOCOLATE CUPS

24 foil candy cup liners

16 ounces white chocolate chips

MOUSSE

4 eggs

Juice and zest from 2 lemons

⅔ cup sugar

1 cup whipping cream

GARNISH (optional)

Lemon zest

Chocolate shavings

Directions

1. In a double boiler over low heat, melt the chocolate. Use a clean paint brush (preferably one that has never been used for paint) to paint the inside of one candy cup liner with chocolate. Paint the bottom and inside edges generously and then place on a cookie sheet. Work quickly and repeat until all the chocolate is used up. Place pan in the freezer.

2. To make the mousse, first separate 3 eggs. Retain the whites for another recipe. In a double boiler, combine the 3 egg yolks plus 1 whole egg with the sugar, lemon juice, and lemon zest. Whisk until mixture thickens into a nice curd. Remove from heat.

3. In a separate bowl, beat the cream until light and fluffy. Fold into the lemon curd, half at a time to keep it light.

4. Remove the chocolate cups from the freezer and carefully peel away the foil liners. Fill each one with a dollop of lemon mousse. Garnish with additional lemon zest and/or chocolate shavings.

Coconut Rice Pudding with Custard Sauce

Ingredients

RICE PUDDING

1 cup rice, uncooked

2 cups coconut milk, divided

⅓ cup brown sugar, packed

¼ teaspoon salt

1 egg, beaten

⅔ cup raisins

1 tablespoon coconut oil

1 teaspoon vanilla

1 teaspoon cinnamon

CUSTARD

2 cups milk

½ cup sugar

6 tablespoons all-purpose gluten-free flour

6 large egg yolks

2 tablespoons vanilla

Directions

1. In a medium saucepan, bring 1½ cups water to a boil. Add rice, stir, cover, reduce heat to low, and simmer for 20 minutes.

2. In a clean saucepan, combine cooked rice, 1½ cups coconut milk, brown sugar, and salt. Cover and cook over medium heat for about 20 minutes. Add remaining ½ cup coconut milk, beaten egg, and raisins, and stir. Cook for another 3 minutes, stirring regularly. Remove from heat and add coconut oil, vanilla, and cinnamon, stirring until incorporated. Cover and refrigerate until ready to serve.

continued on next page

3. Make the custard filling. In a saucepan, bring the milk to a boil with ¼ cup of sugar. Whisk the egg yolks in a separate bowl with the salt and remaining sugar. Sift the flour over the egg mixture and whisk it in until smooth. When the milk boils, slowly whisk ⅓ of it into the egg mixture. Then slowly add the egg mixture to the milk in the saucepan. You must follow these steps to gradually raise the temperature of the eggs. If you add them all at once to the hot milk, they will curdle.

4. Return the saucepan to a medium heat and again bring to a boil, whisking continually. The mixture should begin to thicken. Allow it to boil for another minute. Remove from heat and whisk in the vanilla. Transfer the pastry cream to a bowl. Cover with plastic wrap and refrigerate until very cold, about 2 hours.

5. Layer the rice pudding and custard in shot glasses, small mason jars, or goblets.

Chocolate Espresso Pots de Crème

MAKES 8 SMALL SERVINGS

Ingredients

2 egg yolks

3 tablespoons sugar

⅛ teaspoon salt

6 ounces bittersweet chocolate, chopped

¼ cup cocoa powder

2 teaspoons instant espresso powder

1 cup heavy cream

1 cup whole milk

Chocolate shavings and/or whipped cream for garnish (optional)

Directions

1. In a mixing bowl, whisk together the egg yolks, sugar, and salt.

2. In a double boiler, melt together the chocolate, cocoa powder, and espresso powder. Once melted, remove from heat.

3. In a medium saucepan, heat the cream and milk to almost boiling. Remove from heat and pour in a slow stream over the egg yolk mixture, whisking vigorously. Return mixture to saucepan and simmer, stirring constantly, for about 5 minutes. Remove from heat.

4. Slowly pour the custard mixture over the melted chocolate, whisking vigorously until smooth.

5. Divide between 8 small ramekins or other dishes, cover with plastic wrap, allow to cool for about 10 minutes, and then chill for at least an hour. Just before serving, garnish with chocolate shavings and/or whipped cream, if desired.

Blueberry Trifle

Ingredients

1 pint heavy cream

1 pint blueberries

1 cup crushed gluten-free cookies or
cake pieces

Fruit or nuts, for garnish.

Directions

1. Whip the cream until light and fluffy.
2. Layer the whipped cream, berries, and cookie or cake crumbs in shot glasses. Garnish with more berries, other fruit, or crushed nuts.

{ Sorbets, Popsicles, and Frozen Treats }

Peanut Butter Chocolate Chipwiches   88

Raspberry Sorbet   90

Ice Cream Bars   91

Mango Yogurt Ice Pops   92

Dairy-Free Chocolate Cherry Popsicles   94

Pina Colada Popsicles   96

Mocha Fudgesicles   97

Peanut Butter Chocolate Chipwiches

MAKES ABOUT 20

Ingredients

2¼ cups gluten-free all-purpose
    flour

1 teaspoon xanthan gum

1 teaspoon baking powder

1 teaspoon baking soda

1 teaspoon salt

1 cup butter or coconut oil

1½ cups light brown sugar

2 large eggs

2 teaspoons vanilla extract

12 ounces mini or regular chocolate
    chips

½ cup peanut butter

1 quart ice cream

Directions

1. In a medium bowl, mix together the flour, xanthan gum, baking powder, baking soda, and salt.

2. In a separate bowl, cream together the butter or coconut oil and light brown sugar. Add the eggs, one at a time, and then the vanilla extract, mixing until fully incorporated.

3. Add the dry ingredients into the wet and mix until incorporated. Add 12 ounces (one bag) of mini chocolate chips and stir to combine. Cover the dough and refrigerate for at least an hour.

4. Preheat oven to 350°F. Drop small balls of chilled dough onto greased cookie sheets and bake for about 18 minutes or until just barely golden. Remove from oven, allow pan to cool for about 10 minutes, and then place in the freezer. (If your pans won't fit in the freezer, allow the cookies to cool on racks and then place them in a tin between layers of parchment paper.) Freeze for 4 or more hours.

5. Allow ice cream to soften slightly. Remove from freezer and spread about 1 tablespoon peanut butter on the flat side of a cookie. Place about ¼ cup of ice cream over it and top with another cookie. Wrap in plastic wrap and return to the freezer. Repeat until all chipwiches are made. Serve, or wrap in plastic again and return to freezer.

Raspberry Sorbet

MAKES ABOUT 1 PINT

Ingredients

1 cup water

½ cup sugar

2 cups fresh raspberries

Juice of ½ lemon (around
2 tablespoons)

Directions

1. Combine all ingredients in a saucepan and bring to boil, stirring to avoid burning. Boil 3–4 minutes and then simmer an additional 10 minutes, allowing raspberries to break down.

2. After mix cools, blend well with an immersion blender. Strain through mesh strainer (or through colander lined with cheese-cloth), pressing on the solids.

3. Chill puree for 1 hour or until cold, or quick chill in a bowl of ice and cold water, stirring occasionally for 15–20 minutes (until cold).

4. Freeze puree in ice cream maker according to directions. Garnish with berries if desired. Serve in small glasses or mason jars, in meringue nests (page 119), or in lemon or orange peels that have been halved and hollowed out like bowls.

Ice Cream Bars

MAKES 9 BARS

Ingredients

1 quart ice cream (vanilla, or your favorite flavor)	16 ounces chocolate, chopped
	¼ cup coconut oil

Directions

1. Remove ice cream from freezer to allow to soften a bit. Line the bottom and sides of a 9 x 9-inch baking pan with a large piece of foil or parchment paper, allowing a little extra to hang over the sides. The less the sides of your pan slope, the better.

2. Scoop the ice cream into the pan, cover with plastic wrap, and roll a glass over the plastic to spread the ice cream smoothly. Place pan in freezer and allow to chill overnight.

3. Line a baking sheet with parchment paper. Remove pan of ice cream from freezer, lift ice cream block out of pan, and place on a large cutting board. Cut into 9 even squares, place squares onto lined baking sheet, and return to freezer for about an hour.

4. When ice cream is nearly re-frozen (at least 50 minutes), prepare the chocolate coating. Melt the chocolate and coconut oil together in a double boiler. When fully melted, remove from heat and allow to cool to room temperature, stirring occasionally.

5. Remove ice cream squares from the freezer, spear one square with a fork, dip in the chocolate, and allow excess chocolate to drip off. Return to the lined baking sheet. Repeat with all squares. When all squares are coated, return to the freezer for about half an hour. When chocolate is fully set, serve or wrap individually in plastic to store in freezer.

Mango Yogurt Ice Pops

Ingredients

1 cup mango juice

1 cup fresh or frozen mango chunks

1 (6-ounce) container vanilla yogurt

8 wooden popsicle sticks

Directions

1. Combine all ingredients in blender and blend until smooth. Pour into 8 popsicle molds. Cover, insert popsicle sticks, and freeze at least 2 hours.

2. To serve, run hot water over bottoms of molds to loosen the popsicles. To display at a gathering, arrange popsicles in a bucket of ice or frozen berries. Wrap leftover popsicles individually in plastic wrap and store in a ziplock bag in the freezer.

Dairy-Free Chocolate Cherry Popsicles

MAKES 8 POPSICLES

Ingredients

1 (13.5-ounce) can coconut milk

4 tablespoons honey

1 teaspoon vanilla or almond extract

2 tablespoons coconut oil

1 cup frozen cherries, thawed and chopped into small pieces

3 ounces dark chocolate, finely chopped (about ½ cup)

Directions

1. Combine coconut milk, honey, vanilla, and coconut oil in a blender and blend until smooth and creamy. Pour a little into the bottom of each of 10 popsicle molds. Add a layer of cherry pieces, then chocolate chunks, then more of the liquid. Continue until all ingredients are used, finishing with the liquid. Freeze at least 3 hours.

2. To serve, run hot water over bottoms of molds to loosen the popsicles. To display at a gathering, arrange popsicles in a bucket of ice. Wrap leftover popsicles individually in plastic wrap and store in a ziplock bag in the freezer.

Piña Colada Popsicles

Ingredients

1 (16-ounce) can pineapple chunks
   or 2 cups fresh pineapple chunks
1 cup coconut milk

2 tablespoons honey
3 tablespoons dark rum

Directions

1. Combine all ingredients in a blender and blend until smooth. Pour into popsicle molds and freeze for about 4 hours.

2. To serve, run hot water over bottoms of molds to loosen the popsicles. To display at a gathering, arrange popsicles in a bucket of ice. Wrap leftover popsicles individually in plastic wrap and store in a ziplock bag in the freezer.

Mocha Fudgesicles

Ingredients

2½ cups milk

½ cup sugar

2 tablespoons cornstarch

3 tablespoons cocoa powder

1 tablespoon instant espresso powder

1 tablespoon butter

1 teaspoon vanilla

Directions

1. In a medium saucepan over medium heat, combine milk, sugar, cornstarch, cocoa powder, and espresso powder. Whisk together and bring to a boil. Cook until mixture thickens (about 2 minutes after it begins boiling).

2. Remove from heat, add butter and vanilla and whisk until smooth. Allow to cool and then pour into popsicle molds. Freeze about 6 hours.

3. To serve, run hot water over bottoms of molds to loosen the popsicles. To display at a gathering, arrange popsicles in a bucket of ice. Wrap leftover popsicles individually in plastic wrap and store in a ziplock bag in the freezer.

VARIATION

For an adult fudgesicle, replace the vanilla in the recipe with 2-3 tablespoons Kahlua.

{ Cookies and Candies }

Chocolate-Dipped Macaroons   100

S'mores Bites   101

Fudge Dessert Spoons   104

Chocolate Cheesecake Bonbons in Raspberry Sauce   106

Marshmallow Pops   108

Chocolate-Dipped Macaroons

MAKES ABOUT 24

Ingredients

4 egg whites	½ cup sugar
1 teaspoon vanilla extract	3 cups unsweetened dried shredded
¼ teaspoon almond extract	coconut
¼ teaspoon salt	12 ounces dark chocolate, chopped
1½ tablespoons potato starch	into evenly sized bits

Directions

1. Preheat oven to 325°F. Line two baking sheets with parchment paper or silipat mats.

2. Whisk the egg whites, vanilla extract, almond extract, and salt, until frothy.

3. In a separate bowl, mix together the potato starch and sugar. Add the coconut flakes. Fold this mixture into the egg white mixture.

4. Use a small ice cream scoop to place rounded dollops of the dough onto the lined baking sheet. They won't spread while baking, so they can be placed fairly close. Bake for 15–17 minutes, or until they just begin to turn golden. Remove from oven and transfer to a cooling rack.

5. Melt the chocolate in a double boiler. Dip the bottom of each macaroon in the chocolate and place on the second lined baking sheet. Repeat until all macaroons are dipped.

6. Use a spoon to drizzle more chocolate over the tops if desired. Refrigerate the macaroons for about half an hour to harden. Store between layers of parchment paper in an airtight container.

S'mores Bites

MAKES 12 S'MORES

Ingredients

3 gluten-free graham crackers
3 marshmallows

2 ounces milk chocolate

Directions

1. Break each graham cracker into four sections and place on a baking sheet.
2. Cut each marshmallow into four sections, lengthwise.
3. Place one marshmallow section on each graham cracker piece.
4. Bake at 350°F for 8–10 minutes, until marshmallows begin to brown. Remove and let cool.
5. Melt milk chocolate in a double boiler or saucepan over low heat.
6. Dip each s'more in chocolate and place on baking sheet lined with wax paper.
7. Refrigerate until chocolate sets.

MARSHMALLOWS

Ingredients

1 cup confectioners' sugar
3 envelopes unflavored gelatin
1 cup cold water, divided
2 cups granulated sugar
½ cup light corn syrup
¼ teaspoon salt

2 large egg whites or reconstituted powdered egg whites
1 tablespoon vanilla (or ½ of a scraped vanilla bean or 2 teaspoons almond or mint extract)

Continued on next page

Directions

1. Grease bottom and sides of a 13 x 9 x 2-inch rectangular metal baking pan and dust bottom and sides with confectioners' sugar.

2. In the bowl of a standing electric mixer or in a large bowl sprinkle gelatin over ½ cup cold water, and let stand to soften.

3. In a 3-quart heavy saucepan cook granulated sugar, corn syrup, second ½ cup of cold water, and salt over low heat, stirring with a wooden spoon, until sugar is dissolved. Increase heat to moderate and boil mixture, without stirring, until a candy or digital thermometer registers 240°F, about 12 minutes. Remove pan from heat and pour sugar mixture over gelatin mixture, stirring until gelatin is dissolved.

4. With a standing or a hand-held electric mixer beat mixture on high speed until white, thick, and nearly tripled in volume, about 6 minutes if using standing mixer or about 10 minutes if using hand-held mixer.

5. In separate medium bowl with cleaned beaters beat egg whites (or reconstituted powdered whites) until they just hold stiff peaks. Beat whites and vanilla (or your choice of flavoring) into sugar mixture until just combined. Pour mixture into baking pan. Sift ¼ cup confectioners' sugar evenly over top. Chill marshmallows, uncovered, until firm, at least 3 hours, and up to 1 day.

6. Run a thin knife around edges of pan and invert pan onto a large cutting board. Lifting up one corner of inverted pan, with fingers loosen marshmallow and ease onto cutting board. With a large knife trim edges of marshmallow and cut marshmallow into roughly 1-inch cubes. (An oiled pizza cutter works well here too.) Sift remaining confectioners' sugar back into your now-empty baking pan, and roll the marshmallows through it, on all six sides, before shaking off the excess and packing them away.

GRAHAM CRACKERS

Ingredients

1½ cups blanched almond flour	1 egg
1 tablespoon arrowroot powder	2 tablespoons honey
¼ teaspoon salt	1 teaspoon vanilla
3 tablespoons butter or coconut oil	½ teaspoon cinnamon

Directions

1. Preheat oven to 350°F.
2. Combine all ingredients in a food processor and process until dough begins to stick together.
3. Roll out the dough between two large pieces of parchment paper to ¼ inch thick. Peel away the top piece of parchment, but leave the bottom one in place. Use a sharp knife to cut dough into 6 rectangles that are about 5 x 2½ inches. Score each one into 4 equal parts and use a fork to lightly poke holes in the top. Transfer the parchment paper and crackers to a cookie sheet and back for 8–10 minutes.

Fudge Dessert Spoons

MAKES ABOUT 20 SPOONFULS

Ingredients

1 14-ounce can sweetened condensed milk	½ teaspoon vanilla
12 ounces semisweet chocolate chips	Confectioners' sugar or coarse sea salt and fresh mint leaves, for garnish

Directions

1. Grease an 8 x 8-inch baking pan.
2. In a medium saucepan, heat sweetened condensed milk and chocolate chips. Stir and heat until mixture becomes smooth. Remove from heat and add vanilla.
3. Pour into pan and allow to cool until set. Slice into ½-inch squares. Arrange dessert spoons on serving tray and place a fudge square in each. Dust with confectioners' sugar or sprinkle with sea salt. Garnish with mint leaves, if desired.

Chocolate Cheesecake Bonbons in Raspberry Sauce

MAKES ABOUT 30 BONBONS

Ingredients

BONBONS

1 package cream cheese, softened

2 tablespoons milk

1½ teaspoons vanilla extract

1 cup confectioners' sugar

8 ounces chocolate, chopped

RASPBERRY SAUCE

½ cup sugar

¼ cup water

2 teaspoons cornstarch

2 cups raspberries, fresh or frozen

Directions

1. Line a baking sheet with parchment paper.
2. Beat cream cheese, milk, and vanilla until fluffy. Gradually add confectioners' sugar, beating until combined. Freeze for about 20 minutes, then drop small spoonfuls of the batter onto the baking sheet.
3. Melt chocolate in a double boiler. Use a spoon to drizzle melted chocolate over each cheesecake mound. Refrigerate for another 30 minutes or until chocolate is set.
4. Meanwhile, make the sauce. In a small saucepan over medium heat, whisk together the sugar, water, and cornstarch, simmering until sugar dissolves. Add raspberries and cook, occasionally stirring and mashing down the berries until sauce becomes desired consistency.
5. To serve, arrange dessert spoons on a serving tray. Pour a little sauce in each spoon and then place a bonbon on top.

Marshmallow Pops

MAKES 20 POPS

Ingredients

2 cups chocolate chips

20 large marshmallows

20 popsicle sticks, lollipop sticks, or chopsticks

Sprinkles, coconut flakes, or chopped nuts

Directions

1. Line a baking sheet with parchment paper. Place a marshmallows on the end of each popsicle stick or chopstick.

2. Melt the chocolate in a double boiler. Dip the marshmallows in the melted chocolate, turning to coat. You may want to use a spoon to help coat the marshmallows. Roll in topping of choice and then place on the parchment paper. Once all pops are dipped and rolled, place pan in refrigerator to chill until chocolate is set.

Fruits, Nuts, Meringues, and Other Light Treats

Strawberries 'n Cream   112

Candied Orange Peels   114

Banana Peanut Butter Chocolate Towers   116

Banana Nutella Crepes   118

Meringue Nests with Citrus Curd   119

Almond Pavlovas   122

Mini Chocolate Waffles with Marshmallow-Strawberry
Dipping Sauce   123

Sugar Plums in Citrus Cream   124

Strawberries 'n Cream

Ingredients

1 pound fresh strawberries

8 ounces cream cheese

2 tablespoons butter, softened

1 teaspoon vanilla extract

1 cup confectioners' sugar

2 teaspoons grated lemon zest or chocolate shavings, optional

Directions

1. Wash the strawberries and cut an X in the tip of each one, slicing down to about ½ inch from the hull. Set aside to dry.

2. In a medium bowl using an electric beater, cream together the cream cheese, butter, and vanilla. Add the confectioners' sugar gradually and beat until fully combined. Add the lemon zest and beat another few seconds.

3. Place the cream filling in a pastry bag or ziplock bag with a corner cut out. Squirt a generous portion into the opening of each strawberry. Arrange and serve, or refrigerate for up to a day. Sprinkle with additional lemon zest or dark chocolate shavings if desired.

Candied Orange Peels

Ingredients

3 oranges (peels only)	3 cups water
5 cups sugar, divided	Chocolate chips (optional)

Directions

1. In a large saucepan, bring 3 cups of water to a boil. Wash the orange peels and slice them into strips ¼-inch wide. Place in the boiling water and cook for 15 minutes. Drain into a colander and rinse the peels.
2. In the saucepan whisk together 4 cups of sugar with 3 cups of water. Bring to a boil over medium heat. Add the peels and simmer over low heat for about 45 minutes.
3. Drain into a colander, reserving the syrup for other uses.
4. Place 1 cup of sugar in a bowl and toss the peels until well coated. Transfer peels to a baking sheet lined with aluminum foil. Let stand for 1 to 2 days or until coating is dried. If desired, dip in melted chocolate. Extras can be stored in the freezer for up to 2 months.

Banana Peanut Butter Chocolate Towers

MAKES ABOUT A DOZEN

Ingredients

4 bananas, about 6 inches each

2 cups creamy peanut butter

2 cups semi-sweet chocolate chips

1 cup crushed peanuts

Directions

1. Line a baking sheet with parchment paper.
2. Peel the bananas and slice each one into about 3 pieces, depending on how large the bananas are. Each piece should be about 1½ inches tall. Stand each piece upright and use a straw, chopstick, or corkscrew to hollow out each piece, leaving about ½ inch of banana at the bottom as a base.
3. Melt the chocolate chips in a double boiler, and place the crushed peanuts in a bowl. Dip the bottom of each banana in the melted chocolate and then in the bowl of nuts, and place on the lined cookie sheet. Refrigerate about 10 minutes, or until chocolate is set.
4. Scoop the peanut butter into a pastry bag with a star-shaped tip, or a ziplock bag with one corner snipped off. When chocolate is set, remove bananas from the refrigerator and squirt the peanut butter into each one, adding a swirly dollop on top. Serve immediately, or refrigerate for up to a few hours.

Banana Nutella Crepes

MAKES ABOUT 12

Ingredients

CREPES

2 large eggs

1½ cups milk (cow's, almond, or coconut)

2 tablespoons sugar

1 cup gluten-free all purpose flour

3 tablespoons butter, melted

½ teaspoon vanilla extract

¼ teaspoon almond extract

FILLINGS

½ cup Nutella

2 medium bananas, sliced

Directions

1. In a medium bowl, whisk together the eggs, milk, and sugar. Add the flour, whisking until smooth. Add the melted butter, vanilla extract, and almond extract, whisking just until blended.

2. Heat a 6-inch nonstick skillet. Add about a teaspoon of butter to the pan and swirl around to melt. Ladle about 3 tablespoons of batter into the skillet and tilt the pan until the whole bottom surface is covered with batter. Cook for about a minute, and then use a spatula to lift the edge of the crepe to see if the underside is beginning to brown. If it is, use the spatula to flip the crepe and lightly brown the other side.

3. Layer finished crepes between sheets of parchment paper to keep from sticking together. Repeat until all batter is used, re-buttering the pan as needed.

4. Once crepes are cool enough to handle, divide one in half. Spread a little Nutella over the top surface. Form the crepe into a cone shape and then tuck a few small banana slices inside. Place on serving platter and repeat with remaining crepes.

Meringue Nests with Citrus Curd

MAKES ABOUT 12 NESTS

Ingredients

MERINGUE NESTS

3 egg whites

½ teaspoon vanilla extract

¼ teaspoon cream of tartar

¾ cup sugar

CITRUS CURD

3 egg yolks

⅓ cup sugar

2 tablespoons lemon zest

2 tablespoons fresh orange juice and
  2 tablespoons fresh lemon juice

4 tablespoons unsalted butter, at
  room temperature

Directions

1. Preheat oven to 275°F and line a baking sheet with parchment paper.

2. In a large bowl, beat egg whites, vanilla, and cream of tartar until the mixture forms soft peaks. Add the sugar a little at a time, beating on high until stiff peaks form.

3. Transfer meringue to a pastry bag fitted with a star-shaped or wide round tip. Squirt a small dot of meringue on the paper and then squeeze a thicker circle around it to create a small "nest." Leave about an inch between each one. Bake for 40–45 minutes, or until meringue is set and dry.

4. Meanwhile, make the citrus curd. In a medium saucepan over low heat, combine the egg yolks, sugar, lemon zest, and citrus juice.

continued on next page

Whisk constantly until the mixture thickens (about 7 minutes). Remove from heat and whisk in the butter, about 1 tablespoon at a time. Allow curd to cool slightly, then cover with plastic wrap (placing the plastic directly on the curd so that a skin doesn't form), and refrigerate for 2 hours or longer.

5. To serve, fill each meringue nest with a dollop of curd and arrange on a serving tray. Extra curd can be stored in the refrigerator for up to a week.

Almond Pavlovas

MAKES ABOUT 12

Ingredients

PAVLOVAS

3 egg whites   ¼ teaspoon cream of tartar

½ teaspoon almond extract   ¾ cup sugar

TOPPING

1 cup heavy cream   2 tablespoons honey

½ teaspoon almond extract   ½ cup toasted almond slivers

Directions

1. Preheat oven to 275°F and line a baking sheet with parchment paper

2. In a large bowl, beat egg whites, almond extract, and cream of tartar until the mixture forms soft peaks. Add the sugar a little at a time, beating on high until stiff peaks form.

3. Drop the meringue by tablespoonfuls on the lined cookie sheet, leaving about an inch between each one. Use the back of a spoon to create a slight indentation in the middle of each. Bake for 40–45 minutes, or until meringue is set and dry.

4. Meanwhile, beat the heavy cream in a medium mixing bowl until light and fluffy. Add the almond extract, drizzle in the honey, and mix until incorporated.

5. To serve, be sure meringues are fully cooled. Dollop a little whipped cream on each pavlova and sprinkle with toasted almonds. Arrange on a serving tray.

Mini Chocolate Waffles with Marshmallow-Strawberry Dipping Sauce

Ingredients

WAFFLES

2 cups gluten-free all-purpose flour

2 tablespoons cocoa powder

½ cup sugar

½ teaspoon salt

3 teaspoons baking powder

1 ½ cups milk

2 eggs

4 tablespoons butter, melted

DIPPING SAUCE

½ cup marshmallow fluff

½ cup strawberry jam

Directions

1. Begin heating the waffle iron. In a large mixing bowl, whisk together the flour, cocoa powder, sugar, salt, and baking powder.
2. In a separate bowl, whisk together the milk, eggs, and butter. Pour the wet ingredients into the dry ingredients and stir to combine.
3. When the waffle iron is hot, grease or spray the irons and then ladle on the batter. You'll be making regular-sized waffles and then cutting them into smaller pieces when they're done. Bake 3–5 minutes, or until waffles are golden. Repeat until all batter is used.
4. While waffles are cooling, prepare the dipping sauce simply by mixing together the fluff and jam.
5. Use a small cookie cutter in desired shape to cut the waffles into small pieces. Circles or hearts work better than intricate shapes. Waffle scraps can be used instead of cookies in a trifle (see page 182).
6. Scoop dipping sauce into a small bowl, place on a larger plate, and arrange the waffles on the plate around the bowl.

Sugar Plums in Citrus Cream

MAKES ABOUT A DOZEN DESSERT SPOONS

Ingredients

SUGAR PLUMS

½ cup almonds, hazelnuts, or
    walnuts (or a mix)

¾ cup Medjool dates, prunes, dried
    cranberries, or raisins (or a mix)

1 tablespoon honey

3 tablespoons nut butter (almond,
    peanut, or cashew)

⅛ teaspoon almond extract

⅛ teaspoon vanilla

½ teaspoon cinnamon

⅛ teaspoon cloves

½ cup raw, coarse sugar

CITRUS CREAM

½ cup heavy cream

1 tablespoon honey

½ teaspoon vanilla

1 teaspoon lemon zest (for garnish)

Directions

1. In a food processor, pulse together the dried fruit and nuts. Add the remaining ingredients except for the sugar and pulse until mixture starts to clump together.

2. Roll the dough into small balls and roll in the sugar.

3. To make the citrus cream, beat the heavy cream until it just begins to thicken. Add the honey and vanilla and mix just until combined. Cream should be thickened, but not fluffy. Refrigerate until you're ready to assemble the dessert spoons.

4. To assemble, pour a little cream in each spoon and arrange the spoons on a serving tray. Place a single sugar plum in each spoon, and then sprinkle the lemon zest around it.

{ Index }

All-purpose gluten-free flour mix, xii

Almond
bundt cake with chocolate glaze, 26
pavlovas, 122

Apple
crumb cups, 44
mini apple turnovers, 57

Banana
nutella crepes, 118
peanut butter chocolate towers, 116

Blueberry
trifle, 82
lemon cheesecake bites with blueberry-lemon sauce, 6
lemon-blueberry tartlets, 32

Cake(s)
Almond bundt cake with chocolate glaze, 26
Cranberry pound cake with lemon glaze
Chocolate volcano, 12
Lemon coconut petit fours, 13
Lemon pound cake with fruit and cream
Mini carrot cake,
Pops, 2

Candied orange peels, 114

Caramelized pear pies, 48

Cherry clafoutis, 58

Cherry mascarpone tartlets, 36

Chocolate
almond bundt cake with chocolate glaze, 26
cheesecake bonbons in raspberry sauce, 106
dairy-free chocolate cherry popsicles, 94
dipped macaroons, 100
espresso pots de crème, 81
fudge dessert spoons, 105
lemon mousse in white chocolate cups, 78
mini bundt cakes with sour cream glaze, 19
mini waffles with marshmallow-strawberry dipping sauce, 123
orange cheesecake bites, 10
peanut butter chocolate towers, 116
peanut butter mousse in chocolate cups, 75
raspberry ganache tartlets, 34
s'mores bites, 101
volcano cakes, 12

Chocolate cheesecake bonbons in raspberry sauce, 106

Chocolate espresso pots de crème, 81

Chocolate volcano cakes, 12

Chocolate-dipped macaroons, 100

Chocolate-orange cheesecake bites, 10

Chocolate-raspberry ganache tartlets, 34

Classic whoopie pies, 38

Coconut key lime shooters, 71

Coconut rice pudding with custard sauce, 79

Cranberry pound cake with lemon glaze, 21
Cream puffs, 69
Crepes, banana nutella, 118
Dairy-free chocolate cherry popsicles, 94
Empanaditas, 64
Festive fruit parfaits, 84
Frozen Treats
    dairy-free chocolate cherry popsicles, 94
    ice cream bars, 91
    mango yogurt ice pops, 92
    mocha fudgesicles, 97
    peanut butter chocolate chipwiches, 88
    pina colada popsicles, 96
    raspberry sorbet, 90
Fudge dessert spoons, 104
Galletes
    Rustic plum, 101
    Simple jam, 62
Ginger cream tartlets, 30
Gluten-free piecrust, 48
Graham crackers, 103
Ice cream bars, 91
Lemon
    blueberry tartlets, 32
    cheesecake bites with blueberry-lemon sauce, 6
    coconut petit fours, 13
    mousse in white chocolate cups, 78
    poundcake with fruit and cream, 24
Mango yogurt ice pops, 92
Maple crème brûlée, 68
Marshmallow pops, 108
Marshmallows, 101

Meringue nests with citrus curd, 119
Mini apple turnovers, 57
Mini carrot cakes, 15
Mini chocolate bundt cakes with sour cream glaze, 19
Mini chocolate waffles with marshmallow-strawberry dipping sauce, 123
Mini gingerbread pumpkin cupcakes with spiced cream, 17
Mini pumpkin cheesecakes with gingersnap crust, 8
Mocha fudgesicles, 97
Mocha soufflés, 51
Orange peels, candied, 114
Parfait, festive fruit, 84
Pavlovas, almond, 122
Peanut butter
    cheesecake pops, 5
    chocolate chipwiches, 88
    chocolate towers, 116
    mousse in chocolate cups, 75
Pies
    caramelized pear pies, 48
    classic whoopie pies, 38
    gluten-free piecrust, 48
    maple cream pies, 52
    piecrust, 48
    pumpkin whoopee pies with maple cream filling, 40
    strawberry rhubarb pies, 50
    tollhouse cookie pies, 53
Piecrust, 48
Pina colada popsicles, 96
Pop tarts, 42
Pumpkin whoopee pies with maple cream filling, 40
Raspberry

cheesecake bonbons in
   raspberry sauce, 106
chocolate-raspberry ganache
   tartlets, 34
   peach cobbler, 46
   sorbet, 90
Rhubarb shortcake sliders, 54
Rice pudding, coconut, 79
Rustic plum galletes, 60
S'mores bites, 101
Simple jam galettes, 62
Strawberries
   mini waffles with marshmallow-
      strawberry dipping sauce, 123
   'n cream, 112

rhubarb pies, 50
Sugar plums in citrus cream, 124
Tartlets
   Cherry mascarpone, 36
   Chocolate-raspberry ganache, 34
   Ginger cream, 30
   Lemon-blueberry, 32
Tiramisu cups, 74
Trifle, blueberry, 82
Tollhouse cookie pies, 53
Waffles, mini chocolate, 123
Whoopie Pies
   Classic, 38
   Pumpkin with maple cream
      filling, 40

{ Conversion Charts }

METRIC AND IMPERIAL CONVERSIONS

(These conversions are rounded for convenience)

Ingredient	Cups/Tablespoons/ Teaspoons	Ounces	Grams/Milliliters
Butter	1 cup=16 tablespoons= 2 sticks	8 ounces	230 grams
Cream cheese	1 tablespoon	0.5 ounce	14.5 grams
Cornstarch	1 tablespoon	0.3 ounce	8 grams
Flour, GF all-purpose	1 cup/1 tablespoon	4.5 ounces/0.3 ounce	125 grams/8 grams
Fruit, dried	1 cup	4 ounces	120 grams
Fruits, chopped	1 cup	5 to 7 ounces	145 to 200 grams
Fruits, puréed	1 cup	8.5 ounces	245 grams
Honey, maple syrup, or corn syrup	1 tablespoon	.75 ounce	20 grams
Liquids: cream, milk, water, or juice	1 cup	8 fluid ounces	240 milliliters
Oats	1 cup	5.5 ounces	150 grams
Salt	1 teaspoon	0.2 ounce	6 grams
Spices: cinnamon, cloves, ginger, or nutmeg (ground)	1 teaspoon	0.2 ounce	5 milliliters
Sugar, brown, firmly packed	1 cup	7 ounces	200 grams
Sugar, white	1 cup/1 tablespoon	7 ounces/0.5 ounce	200 grams/12.5 grams
Vanilla extract	1 teaspoon	0.2 ounce	4 grams

Gluten-Free Miniature Desserts

OVEN TEMPERATURES

Fahrenheit	Celsius	Gas Mark
225°	110°	¼
250°	120°	½
275°	140°	1
300°	150°	2
325°	160°	3
350°	180°	4
375°	190°	5
400°	200°	6
425°	220°	7
450°	230°	8